Population and the Planet

Understanding the issues

by
Dermot Grenham

All booklets are published thanks to the generous support of the members of the Catholic Truth Society

CATHOLIC TRUTH SOCIETY
PUBLISHERS TO THE HOLY SEE

Contents

Seven billion people just like you and me 3

Some demographic background 6

The history of population concerns 14

The Catholic Church's position on the
population question 21

Dealing with concerns about overpopulation 35

Some demographic terminology 57

A two-sided debate 62

Seven billion people just like you and me

"The human race, to which so many of my readers belong..."[1] so started G. K. Chesterton one of his books. It's unlikely that there will be any non-human readers of this booklet, which is just as well as it is all about the human race, our race: its past, for which we ought to be on the whole grateful, its present, which we ought to live with passion, and its future, about which we ought to be optimistic.[2]

At some point during the second half of 2011 or possibly early in 2012 planet Earth will play host to seven billion people.[3] That's seven billion people just like you and me – same desires, same hopes, and same fears. For some this will be a reason to celebrate as they will be aware that people are generally living longer, healthier lives. For others, however, it will be a cause for great concern, as they think that such an enormous population will use up the Earth's finite resources and destroy the environment. The debate about the advantages and disadvantages of large and growing populations has a long history and goes back to way before Malthus. He was writing at the end of the 18th and beginning of the 19th century. It's Malthus' name which is most often associated with dire predictions about the consequences of population growth. As the Earth's population continues to expand at least for the next few decades the debate will undoubtedly continue. The Catholic Church has a keen interest in this debate because she is concerned about each and every woman and man as Pope John Paul II expressed in 1979:

"Man as *willed* by God, as chosen by him from eternity and called, destined for grace and glory - this is *each* man, *the most concrete* man, *the most real*; this is man in all the fullness of the mystery in which he has become a sharer in Jesus Christ, the mystery in which each one of the four thousand million human beings living on our planet has become a sharer from the moment he is conceived beneath the heart of his mother... Man is the primary route that the Church must travel in fulfilling her mission: he is the primary and fundamental way for the Church..."[4]

This booklet provides an explanation of the history and status of the population debate, distinguishes between genuine concerns and simple scaremongering and explains the Catholic Church's teaching regarding population issues. It has deliberately been written in non-technical language to make it accessible to as wide a readership as possible and also because most of the debate takes place in non-technical language. For those interested, brief explanations of some of the technical terminology used and a discussion of how the UN and other organisations produce population projections are included in the final main section of this booklet.

There are two population debates going on at present. The first is about the size and growth of the human population and whether this is sustainable at its present let alone future level. The second is about the ageing populations currently being experienced in most developed countries and not a few developing countries and the impact this will have on their society and economy.

I will start off by giving some demographic background. This will include a brief history of the population of the World and a look at some of the key demographic issues. With this background I will then look at what key writers have written about population through the ages to show that concerns about overpopulation stretch back for a very long time. I will then look at the Catholic Church's teaching on population related issues. The final section will cover the main areas of the debate about population growth such as its impact of economic development and the environment.

Some demographic background

Demography is the study of populations particularly with respect to their size, structure and development. It focuses on mortality, fertility and migration as these are the key processes affecting how population size changes over time. Assumptions about these processes are used in making population projections.

History and future of the world's population

The graph on the following page shows the history of the world's population over the past 250 years.[5]

While it took many thousands of years for the Earth's population to reach 2 billion (around 1930), the global population has reached successive billions increasingly faster. Growing from 2 to 3 billion took around 33 years, and from 3 to 4 billion took a further 14 years. It will have taken around 13 years for the population to increase from 6 billion to 7 but this is where the trend changes. Not only has the rate of increase in the world's population slowed down (which started happening in the early 1970s) but the actual annual increase in the population is falling. Current UN projections estimate that the world's population in the middle of the 21st century will be just over 9 billion and will be around 10 billion at the end of the current century.

History and Future of the World's Population

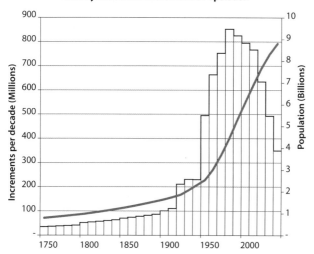

The bars show increments as measured on the left hand axis. The line shows the global population as measured on the right hand axis. UN Population Division (1999) *The World at Six Billion*.

Causes of global population growth

The fundamental cause of the large increase in the global population over the past couple of centuries has been the reduction in death rates, particularly among the under 5s. According to the UN[6], average life expectancy worldwide is now around 68 years compared to 50 years half a century ago. Although these averages hide wide disparities, life expectancy has increased in all countries over the past 50 years with only a couple of exceptions. Most countries have moved or are moving, except in some countries currently badly affected by HIV/AIDS, from a position where mortality was high, especially at very young ages and due to communicable diseases, wars and famines, to a situation where mortality rates are relatively low, with life expectancies at birth of over 60.

At the same time, most countries have moved or are moving from a position where fertility was high to a position where fertility is low. This combination of declining mortality and fertility is known as the demographic transition and is illustrated in the diagram on the following page. All countries have at least started along the path of the demographic transition even if they have not completed it. During the demographic transition mortality rates usually fall earlier and faster than fertility rates and it is this which gives rise to population growth. The longer it takes for fertility to fall to the same level as the mortality rates the more population growth there will be. Therefore, in the words of Nicholas Eberstadt, the world's population is growing, "not because people are breeding like rabbits but that they are no longer dying like flies".[7]

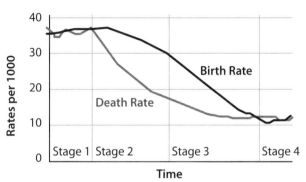

The Demographic transition.

Population decline

Most of the 3 billion or so increase in population over the rest of the 21st century is projected to take place in the less and least developed countries. In most of the more developed countries population is expected to fall and has already started doing so in some countries, such as Russia. Countries with low birth rates and high levels of emigration are particularly exposed to population decline. In a number of countries, for example, Italy, mortality rates are higher than birth rates and it is only immigration which is preventing the population declining. As a consequence, developing countries will continue to make up an increasing proportion of the world's population. This increased population relative to the currently developed countries is likely to bring with it, as we are already seeing in the case of some of the BRICs (Brazil, Russia, India and China), greater influence in global affairs. The other side of the coin though is that developed countries are likely to see their influence diminish along with their populations.

A sign of whether, in the long run a country's population will grow or decline is whether its fertility rate is higher or lower than the "replacement rate". The replacement rate is the number of children that women, on average, need to have for the population to remain the same size, over the long term. This rate is normally around 2.1 children per woman. It is slightly greater than 2 first of all to allow for those women who do not survive to the end of their reproductive years. A second reason why it is greater than 2 is that in almost all populations more boys are born than girls, typically around 105 boys for every 100 girls. Therefore, to ensure that the number of females remains the same (and after all, it is women who give birth) there has to be, on average, slightly more than 2 children born per woman. Almost all developed countries and an increasing number of developing countries have a fertility rate well below the replacement rate.

Population ageing

At the same time as the population of the world is projected to get larger it is also projected to get older. This is a necessary consequence of the demographic transition. Current population ageing is mainly due to lower birth rates. Increased life expectancy also contributes but not so significantly at present. If birth rates stop falling then further increases in life expectancy will have a larger impact on population ageing.

Population ageing can start to be a serious problem if there are not enough productive people to support the increasing number of non-productive people in a society. It is not possible to set an age at which people stop being productive and become non-productive, this will depend very much on the individual and on his or her health, training and skills. It will also depend on how easy a society makes it for older people to continue in the labour force. In countries where the state provides a pension, the debate is often framed in terms of the age at which this pension is paid. In the UK this is currently 65 for men and 60 rising to 65 for women. However, as people live longer and are generally healthier for longer, it would not seem unreasonable, and in fact would seem to be in line with the Church's teaching on the need for everyone to contribute to the Common Good, that people should work longer, assuming of course that appropriate employment opportunities are available to them. An ageing population could be a bigger problem in societies with little by way of social protection for elderly people as the responsibility for looking after parents will fall directly upon the few children and grandchildren that they have.

Faced with an ageing population, a society may be tempted to allow euthanasia to a great or lesser extent as a way of reducing the burden of paying pensions and healthcare for the elderly. It is probably no coincidence that increased calls for legalising euthanasia have arisen within societies where there is already a certain level of pessimism about the future. It is probably the same pessimism which led to a reduction in birth rates in the first place.

The impact of government population policies

As an example of the dangers inherent in governments interfering too heavy-handedly in demographic processes, one can look at the example of China. As a result of the Chinese government's one child policy (which is currently closer to a one and a half child policy), a cultural preference among Chinese couples for having sons, and access to sex-selective abortion, there are currently around 120 boys born for every 100 girls[8] the highest level in the world. This will have the effect of pushing up the replacement rate for China to around 2.3

and therefore will cause China to age more rapidly than it would have done with a more normal sex ratio at birth. The imbalance of males over females at birth is compounded by the neglect of young girls leading to the phenomenon of "missing women"[9]. This affects not only China but also India and some other countries with a strong cultural preference for sons and worldwide it has been estimated that there are between 50 and 100 million missing women. Among the problems that the Chinese are storing up for themselves as a result of their government's demographic policy is the social consequences of increasingly large number of males who are unable to find brides. Another cultural consequence is that within a couple of generations relations such as aunts, uncles and cousins will become increasingly rare.

The history of population concerns

The name of Reverend Thomas Malthus, an Anglican clergyman, is closely associated with pessimistic views about the effects of an increasing population. Current day pessimists are often referred to as neo-Malthusians on account of the similarity of outlook if not always an identical line of argument. However, Malthus was not the first to worry about the impact of too many people.

Ancient times

Plato and Aristotle in their books 'Laws' and 'Politics' respectively, discussed the ideal size of a population. Tertullian, an early Christian writer, got carried away in his book 'De Anima' when arguing against the theory of the transmigration of souls, and wrote "What most frequently meets our view (and occasions complaint), is our teeming population: our numbers are burdensome to the world, which can hardly supply us from its natural elements; our wants grow more and more keen, and our complaints more bitter in all mouths, whilst Nature fails in affording us her usual sustenance. In very deed, pestilence, and famine, and wars, and earthquakes have to be regarded as a remedy for nations, as the means of pruning the luxuriance of the human race."[10] Clearly a Malthusian before his time.

The Middle Ages

Machiavelli writing in the early 16th century said more or less the same in his book 'Discourses on the First Decade of Titus Livius' although he sees events such as floods and plagues as having a moral as well as an economic effect on the population: "So likewise as regards that composite body the human race, when every province of the world so teems with inhabitants that they can neither subsist where they are nor remove elsewhere, every region being equally crowded and over-peopled, and when human craft and wickedness have reached their highest pitch, it must needs come about that the world will purge herself in one or another of these three ways [floods, plagues, and famines], to the end that men, becoming few and contrite, may amend their lives and live with more convenience."[11]

The Enlightenment

However, during the 17th and 18th centuries there tended to be more concern about underpopulation than overpopulation and "populousness" was praised and encouraged by writers such as David Hume and Jean-Jacques Rousseau who saw a growing population as a proof of good government.

Malthus

Malthus who wrote the first version of his famous 'Essay on the Principle of Population'[12] in 1798 was reacting to the views of writers such as Godwin and Condorcet that, as human knowledge increased it would be possible to reach a stage of natural human perfection. Malthus' simple put down to this was to state that, to the extent that living conditions improved parents would have more children so that they will end up back where they started or even worse off or, in Malthus' own, more dramatic, words: "The power of population is so superior to the power in the earth to produce subsistence for man, that premature death must in some shape or other visit the human race. The vices of mankind are active and able ministers of depopulation. They are the precursors in the great army of destruction; and often finish the dreadful work themselves. But should they fail in this war of extermination, sickly seasons, epidemics, pestilence, and plague, advance in terrific array, and sweep off their thousands and ten thousands. Should success be still incomplete, gigantic inevitable famine stalks in the rear, and with one mighty blow levels the population with the food of the world." His basic theory was that food production could only increase in arithmetic progression (1, 2, 3, 4,...) while population would, if not checked, increase in geometric progression (1, 2, 4, 8,...) so sooner or later the population would outstrip the food available.

The regular recurrence of the Malthusian arguments, in spite of the general although unfortunately not universal improvement in human well-being, is in itself a strong proof that they are more of a reaction to temporary symptoms of malaise rather than a fundamental argument against population growth. However, some of those who share Malthus' pessimism would argue that, while previous claims of imminent disaster were clearly overblown the pessimists are right this time. I'll come back to this when I deal with specific areas of concern.

Followers and early critics of Malthus

The Malthusian ideas became, and remain, closely linked up with the evolutionary ideas of Charles Darwin and the eugenic ideas of Francis Galton. As a result, arguments about the need to reduce population growth rates, while framed in terms of a desire to enable those that are born to live better lives, often disguise a desire to see fewer of those who are considered less fit to live. As most of the future population growth of the world will take place in developing countries, programmes aimed at slowing population growth, most of which are designed and funded by developed countries, will clearly be aimed at reducing the number of those living in poorer countries relative to those in developed countries. It is easy to see this as a reaction to the concern that the growing numbers of poorer people will, out of justice, demand a greater share of the world's riches. This view of the anti-poor undertones of the Malthusian theory was shared by both Marx and Engels and the latter expressed his disagreement in terms that are similar to those used by the more current opponents to neo-Malthusian ideas. "The area of land is limited", Engels wrote, "– that is perfectly true. But the labour power to be employed on this area increases together with the population; and even if we assume that the increase of output associated with this increase of labour is not always proportionate to the latter, there still remains a third element – which the economists, however, never consider as important – namely, science, the progress of which is just as limitless and at least as rapid as that of population."[13]

The 20th century: neo-Malthusians and their opponents

Malthusian ideas went out of fashion to quite a large extent in the first half of the 20th century partly because, during this period, which included the years of the Great Depression between the two World Wars, there was concern about the possibility of population decline as discussed in books with titles such as 'Twilight of Parenthood'. However, very soon after the Second World War, concerns about the impact of population growth on the environment started surfacing and these led in 1968 to the publication by Paul Ehrlich, one of the best known current neo-Malthusians, of 'The Population Bomb'. Ehrlich opened his book with the statement "The battle to feed all of humanity is over. In the 1970s hundreds of millions of people will starve to death in spite of any crash programs embarked upon now. At this late date nothing can prevent a substantial increase in the world death rate..."[14] In spite of the fact that this and the other predictions made in the book have not come to pass Ehrlich argues that all he got wrong was the timing. During the 1960s and 1970s concerns over population growth gathered momentum and became more mainstream. Population control programmes were imposed in India in 1976 when it introduced a compulsory sterilisation programme and in China in the late 1970s with its one child policy. The Indian programme was relatively short-lived and seems to have been a contributory factor in the fall of Indira Gandhi's government. The Chinese one child policy is still in place although it has gone through various changes since its implementation and currently is a "one and a half" child policy.

In the 1980s and 1990s there were new challenges to the neo-Malthusian arguments based on the observation that while theoretically an increasing population could cause problems such as those described by Paul Ehrlich, and in the short term and in some places it may have done, the actual evidence demonstrated that over the longer term life is getting better for most people on the planet. Two of the best known proponents of this revisionist view are Julian Simon, author of 'The Ultimate Resource' and 'The Ultimate Resource 2', and Bjorn Lomborg, author of 'The Skeptical Environmentalist'. These two authors were following in the footsteps of Colin Clark and Ester Boserup who demonstrated that the world could feed a population vastly greater than we currently have and that population pressure can actually be a driving force for improvements in food production technology and practices.

As a counter balance to the quotation from Malthus included above here is a much more optimistic quote from Simon's 'The Ultimate Resource 2': "Adding more people causes problems, but people are also the means to solve these problems. The main fuel to speed our progress is our stock of knowledge, and the brake is our lack of imagination. The ultimate resource is people - skilled, spirited, and hopeful people who will exert their wills and imaginations for their own benefit, and inevitably they will benefit not only themselves but the rest of us as well."[15]

The Catholic Church's position on the population question

The Church's teaching on population matters, as regards the issue of population growth, goes back at least to Blessed John XXIII. Papal teaching in this area challenges the basis of the concerns over population growth, describes how solutions can be found, sets criteria for the role of governments, and discusses responsible parenthood and the place of large families. It also covers issues caused by the low birth rates currently being experienced in many countries. The Church honours childbearing and rearing as a sharing in God's creative power and while recognising the very real difficulties and challenges associated with giving birth and bringing up children it sees these in a positive light rather than as mere "domestic drudgery and the childbirth treadmill"[16].

The Church's position on population growth

In his 1961 encyclical 'Mater et Magistra', Blessed John XXIII set out what have since become the main lines of the Church's teaching regarding population growth. He acknowledged that there was widespread concern, at both a global level and with respect to poor countries in particular, that food production and economic development would not keep pace with population growth and that, as a consequence population control was being put forward as a solution. However, the Pope pointed out that such concerns were based on "such unreliable and controversial data that they can only be of very uncertain validity." The Pope expressed confidence that God's providence and man's intelligence would be able to solve the problems caused by population growth through scientific and technical effort and not through expedients that "offend the moral order and attack life at its very source" as a result of being based on an "utterly materialistic conception of human beings and their lives". The very real scourge of poverty was due to "deficient economic and social organisation and a lack of effective solidarity among people." Technological progress on its own would not solve this problem; any real solution would have to promote "social and economic progress both of individuals and of the whole of human society" and "true human values." The Pope called for "worldwide co-operation among men, with a view to a fruitful and well-regulated interchange of useful knowledge, capital and manpower."

Pope Paul VI in 'Populorum Progressio' wrote in a similar vein that population growth has made development more difficult and this has tempted people to apply drastic remedies to reduce the birth rate. While granting governments the right to intervene to instruct their citizens he stated that they must act within the dictates of the moral law and leave married couple free to decide how many children to have. To take away this freedom from couples would be to take away human dignity. At the same time he stressed that while parents have to decide upon how many children they will have, following their conscience and God's law, they have to bear in mind their obligations to their existing children and to the community and, at the same time, trust in God.

Blessed John Paul II in 'Evangelium Vitae' complained that rather than responsible and effective solutions being found to the serious demographic, family and social problems, false and deceptive solutions were being proposed which were opposed to the truth and good of persons and nations. In very chilling words he described how "The Pharaoh of old, haunted by the presence and increase of the children of Israel, submitted them to every kind of oppression and ordered that every male child born of the Hebrew women was to be killed (cf. *Ex* 1:7-22). Today not a few of the powerful of the earth act in the same way. They too are haunted by the current demographic growth, and fear that the most prolific and poorest peoples represent a threat for the well-being and peace of their own countries. Consequently, rather than wishing to face and solve these serious problems with respect for the dignity of individuals and families and for every person's inviolable right to life, they prefer to promote and impose by whatever means a massive programme of birth control. Even the economic help which they would be ready to give is unjustly made conditional on the acceptance of an anti-birth policy." He had previously pointed out in 'Sollicitudo Rei Socialis' that population control campaigns in developing countries are often required by donors before aid is granted. As a result couples, especially the poorest, are put under pressure to submit to this oppression.

The role of Governments

As Paul VI pointed out, the Church accepts that governments may legitimately seek to influence couples regarding the number of children they choose to have while leaving the final decision up to them. This can work in both directions as, at certain times, governments may wish to encourage a slower population growth rate or, as is currently the case in Russia, they may wish to encourage an increase.

Governments and other national and international bodies should, however, limit themselves to providing objective and reliable information on which couples may base their decisions. Blessed John Paul II stated firmly in 'Familiaris Consortio' that "...the Church condemns as a grave offence against human dignity and justice all those activities of governments or other public authorities which attempt to limit in any way the freedom of couples in deciding about children. Consequently, any violence applied by such authorities in favour of contraception or, still worse, of sterilization and procured abortion, must be altogether condemned and forcefully rejected. Likewise to be denounced as gravely unjust are cases where, in international relations, economic help given for the advancement of peoples is made conditional on programs of contraception, sterilization and procured abortion."

The 'Catechism of the Catholic Church' sums up the Church's position in paragraph 2372 as follows:

"The state has a responsibility for its citizens' well-being. In this capacity it is legitimate for it to intervene to orient the demography of the population. This can be done by means of objective and respectful information, but certainly not by authoritarian, coercive measures. The state may not legitimately usurp the initiative of spouses, who have the primary responsibility for the procreation and education of their children. It is not authorized to intervene in this area with means contrary to the moral law."

Governments have generally found that while measures to reduce birth rates have often been successful, trying to increase birth rates tends to be a much harder task.

Responsible parenthood

The Church's teaching on responsible parenthood was explained in the Second Vatican Council document 'Gaudium et Spes': "Parents should regard as their proper mission the task of transmitting human life and educating those to whom it has been transmitted. They should realize that they are thereby co-operators with the love of God the Creator, and are, so to speak, the interpreters of that love. Thus they will fulfil their task with human and Christian responsibility, and, with docile reverence toward God, will make decisions by common counsel and effort. Let them thoughtfully take into account both their own welfare and that of their children, those already born and those which the future may bring. For this accounting they need to reckon with both the material and the spiritual conditions of the times as well as of their state in life. Finally, they should consult the interests of the family group, of temporal society, and of the Church herself."[17]

Thus it is certainly not true to say, as some opponents of the Catholic Church's teaching in this area maintain, that the Church promotes unlimited procreation. At times, responsible parenthood would require that couples avoid having any more children while in some situations, responsible parenthood would mean that couples, prudently and generously, should have more children while in other situations it would mean that they should avoid having children, at least for a time.

Pope Paul VI in his encyclical 'Humane Vitae' provided a detailed explanation of what responsible parenthood means in a number of areas including the biological, social and theological. The human mind is able discern the laws that apply to the human person and in the light of these our reason needs to exert control over our innate drives and emotions. Responsible parenthood can lead some parents to decide to have more children while others would be acting responsibly where, for serious reasons and with due respect to moral precepts, they decide not to have additional children for either a certain or an indefinite period of time. Couples need to remember that they do not act in isolation but should recognise their duties toward God, themselves, their families and human society. They are not free to act as they choose in the service of transmitting life, as if it were wholly up to them to decide what the right course to follow is. On the contrary, they are bound to ensure that what they do corresponds to the will of God the Creator.

Blessed John Paul II summarised the Church's understanding of responsible parenthood in his book 'Crossing the Threshold of Hope':

"Obviously, the opposite of the culture of death is not and cannot be a program of irresponsible global population growth. *The rate of population growth needs to be taken into consideration*. The right path is that which the Church calls *responsible parenthood*; this is taught by the Church's family counselling programs. Responsible parenthood is the necessary condition for human love, and it is also the necessary condition for authentic conjugal love, because love cannot be irresponsible. Its beauty is the fruit of responsibility. When love is truly responsible, it is also truly free."[18]

Large families

However, a misunderstood reading of responsible parenthood could have the unintended consequence of putting people off having large families. This is not what the Church wants. In 1958, Pope Pius XII said, in an address to representatives of large families in Italy:

"But you do not represent just any families at all; you are and represent large families, those most blessed by God and specially loved and prized by the Church as its most precious treasures. For these families offer particularly clear testimony to three things that serve to assure the world of the truth of the Church's doctrine and the soundness of its practice, and that rebound, through good example, to the great benefit of all other families and of civil society itself. Wherever you find large families in great numbers, they point to: the physical and moral health of a Christian people; a living faith in God and trust in His Providence; the fruitful and joyful holiness of Catholic marriage.

As for you, parents and children of large families, keep on giving a serene and firm testimony of your trust in divine Providence, and be assured that He will not fail to repay you with the testimony of His daily help and, whenever necessary, with those extraordinary helps that many of you have been happy to experience already."

For many families responsible parenthood may mean that they ought to have more children than they might otherwise have. It is worth noting, though, that what is meant by a large family changes over time and is culturally conditioned. In many developed countries families with 3 children would be considered large while in poorer countries this could well be considered a relatively small family. One also needs to distinguish between having many children in a country with high infant and child mortality rates such that a high proportion would be expected to die young and having many children where most would be expected to survive to adulthood.

Low birth rates

Benedict XVI in 'Caritas in Veritate' stated that "...formerly prosperous nations are presently passing through a phase of uncertainty and in some cases decline, precisely because of their falling birth rates; this has become a crucial problem for highly affluent societies. The decline in births, falling at times beneath the so-called "replacement level", also puts a strain on social welfare systems, increases their cost, eats into savings and hence the financial resources needed for investment, reduces the availability of qualified labourers, and narrows the "brain pool" upon which nations can draw for their needs. Furthermore, smaller and at times miniscule families run the risk of impoverishing social relations, and failing to ensure effective forms of solidarity. These situations are symptomatic of scant confidence in the future and moral weariness. It is thus becoming a social and even economic necessity once more to hold up to future generations the beauty of marriage and the family, and the fact that these institutions correspond to the deepest needs and dignity of the person. In view of this, States are called to enact policies promoting the centrality and the integrity of the family founded on marriage between a man and a woman, the primary vital cell of society, and to assume responsibility for its economic and fiscal needs, while respecting its essentially relational character."

The Church therefore points out the danger in having too low a birth rate although this is as much a symptom of a deeper existential problem as it is the cause of further problems. The Church itself suffers as a result of low birth rates as fewer men and women are available to respond to calls to vocations to the priesthood and the religious life. In 2004, Archbishop Csaba Ternyak, Secretary of the Congregation for the Clergy, said that although the number of priests in the world is on the rise, where populations are declining so are the number of priests. He stated that the drop in vocations in some Western countries "corresponds to the progressive aging of the local population, the troublesome phenomenon of the drop in birth rates, and finally to the cultural phenomenon of the increase in secularism." At the same time, he said that a growth in the clergy is occurring, especially on the younger continents, "where procreation is still significant and where the culture has been less affected by religious crisis."[19]

The population question and the culture of life

When all is said and done, how people view the potential impact of population growth tends to spring from a deeper view they have of the value of human life, any human life. As Blessed John Paul II said in 'Familiaris Consortio': "Scientific and technical progress, which contemporary man is continually expanding in his dominion over nature, not only offers the hope of creating a new and better humanity, but also causes ever greater anxiety regarding the future. Some ask themselves if it is a good thing to be alive or if it would be better never to have been born; they doubt therefore if it is right to bring others into life when perhaps they will curse their existence in a cruel world with unforeseeable terrors. Others consider themselves to be the only ones for whom the advantages of technology are intended and they exclude others by imposing on them contraceptives or even worse means. Still others, imprisoned in a consumer mentality and whose sole concern is to bring about a continual growth of material goods, finish by ceasing to understand, and thus by refusing, the spiritual riches of a new human life. The ultimate reason for these mentalities is the absence in people's hearts of God, whose love alone is stronger than all the world's fears and can conquer them. Thus an anti-life mentality is born, as can be seen in many current issues: one thinks, for example, of a certain panic deriving from the studies of ecologists and futurologists on population growth, which sometimes exaggerate the danger of demographic increase to the quality of life. But the Church firmly believes that human life, even if weak and suffering, is always a splendid gift of God's goodness. Against the pessimism and selfishness which cast a shadow over the world, the Church stands for life: in each human life she sees the splendour of that "Yes," that "Amen," who is Christ Himself. To the "No" which assails and afflicts the world, she replies with this living "Yes," thus defending the human person and the world from all who plot against and harm life."[20]

Reproductive health

It is not possible to discuss population issues without dealing with the topic of reproductive health especially in the context of developing countries. The Catholic Church is as committed to improving women and men's reproductive health as anyone else. The problem is that the term reproductive health means different things to different people. For some people, reproductive health includes making contraception (by which generally only so called 'modern methods' are meant) and abortion freely available whereas for the Church neither artificial contraception nor abortion are morally acceptable. The Church's stance has been criticised as uncaring and dogmatic. However, any human rights based approach to determining what is right and wrong will appear uncaring and dogmatic as by definition such an approach focuses on principles rather than on consequences.

The Church's teaching on contraception and abortion is well known although the underlying reasons for this are less well known, even by many Catholics. The teaching is demanding but at the same time positive and in tune with the deepest desires of women and men. It needs to be put across with greater confidence and credibility. Methods of artificial contraception and abortion are not going to be uninvented. What is required is to make them unwanted as a result of the free choice of women and men.

One of the justifications for promoting ready access to artificial contraception is that many women, especially in poorer countries, are married and do not want to have another child either at all or at least not now. This is called the 'unmet need' for contraception. However, this concept is not without problems, is it really an unmet need for contraception or rather an unmet need for safe pregnancies, healthcare, especially for children, and education?

The introduction and promotion of artificial contraception while it may be a response to changing cultural views, can also have a major impact on the culture and human behaviour. In 'Humanae Vitae', Paul VI described some of the negative impacts of making artificial contraception available. These included making marital infidelity easier and generally lowering moral standards. He also foresaw that the relationship between men and women would change as a consequence of husbands not treating their wives with the reverence due to them and seeing in them instruments for pleasure rather than a partner to be treated with care and affection. In places where women are already treated without sufficient respect and reverence, making contraception available is going to do nothing to change this and instead, by reducing the risk of pregnancy, remove one of the factors that may be helping to prevent men's behaviour becoming even worse.

Dealing with concerns about overpopulation

In this section I will discuss some of the concerns raised by fears of 'overpopulation' and 'rapid population growth' and how to address them. The fundamental argument is that while the population of the world has expanded significantly over the past 200 hundred years or so, the average level of well-being has also increased although large numbers of people are still to fully benefit from this. There is no reason, in principle, to suppose that it will not be possible to continue improving the lot of humanity even with a much larger population. Those who are concerned about overpopulation think that we have been lucky so far and that with an ever-increasing population our luck just has to run out sometime. But why should this be?

This is not to say that a larger population, whether at a global, national or family level does not bring problems. Nor is it to deny that some of the problems that people are facing could not be more easily dealt with if there were fewer of them. However, human experience is that there will always be problems of one sort or another no matter how big or small the population; after all we will never build heaven on earth. Trying to reduce the size of the Earth's population or its growth rate by more or less coercive methods or by changing the culture of peoples to make them want fewer children may have some short term gains in terms of economic development but at what human, or social cost? And there is no guarantee that a smaller population or a slower population growth rate will lead to faster economic development.

This section is not aiming to prove that a larger population will necessarily lead to greater economic or social development. Demography is just one of the many social, cultural, economic and political variables that influence how a society develops. However, to think that by reducing birth rates one will automatically speed up development, at the very least demonstrates a great lack of imagination.

The links between population growth and economic development are technical issues and therefore not part of the magisterium of the Catholic Church. Therefore Catholics are free to make their own assessment of the actual and potential linkages. However, as the Catechism of the Catholic Church points out, any solutions to developmental problem arising from population growth have to be morally acceptable.[21]

The key areas of the debate over the impact of large populations are: space, food, mineral resources, energy, water, economic development and the environment, including climate change. I will deal with each of these in turn.

Space

This is the most basic and crudest of the concerns about overpopulation as it expresses the worry that there will simply not be enough room for everybody. In my experience, if you ask someone how many people there are in the world they will give a fairly accurate answer, usually somewhere around 7 billion. However, if you then ask them how big the world is they are unlikely to have much of a clue. If one does not know how big the world is, how can one argue that there is not enough room? In fact, the amount of land on the planet is approximately 150 million km² or 58 million miles². This means that with 7 billion people on the planet each person could have 21,429m² or 231,000ft² to themselves. Admittedly some of this would not be particularly hospitable, although it is amazing how human beings have managed to live in some of the most difficult terrains on Earth. The example of Easter Island is relevant here. While this is often put forward as an example of a population that outgrew its environment what is equally striking is how long the people managed to survive there before the population collapsed.

Another way of thinking about the relationship between the size of the world's population and the size of the world is to consider that the whole of the world's population could fit on the Isle of Man (a small island of

572km² or 221miles² between Great Britain and Ireland). Admittedly it would be a bit of a crush. Fortunately, as a very high proportion of the world's population is currently made up of young people in developing countries these take up much less room than the larger, not to say obese, populations of the richer countries. And if everyone did squeeze on to the Isle of Man then the rest of the world would be completely empty of people!

Most of the future increase in the world's population will take place in urban areas and already just over half of the world's population are urbanised. This means that more people are living in less space compared to populations living in rural areas. Also, in theory, it is easier to provide services and amenities to urban populations although not all countries have managed to do this for one reason or another.

In 1971, following a visit to New Delhi, Paul Ehrlich wrote the following:

"The streets seemed alive with people. People eating, people washing, people sleeping. People visiting, arguing, screaming. People thrusting their hands through the taxi window, begging. People defecating and urinating. People clinging to buses. People herding animals. People, people, people, people. As we moved slowly through the mob, the dust, noise, heat and cooking fires gave the scene a hellish aspect. Would we ever get to our hotel...? Since that night I have known the feel of overpopulation."[22]

However, Mahmood Mamdani, Professor and Director of the Makerere Institute of Social Research at Makerere University, Kampala, Uganda, and the Herbert Lehman Professor of Government at Columbia University, New York wrote in response that:

"The fact is that a hot summer night on Broadway in New York or Piccadilly Circus in London would put Ehrlich in the midst of a far larger crowd. Yet such an experience would not spur him to comment with grave concern about 'overpopulation.' On the other hand, with a little more concern and a little less fear he would have realized that what disturbed him about the crowd in Delhi was not its numbers, but its 'quality'-that is, its poverty. To talk, as Ehrlich does, of 'overpopulation' is to say to people: you are poor because you are too many. People are not poor because they have large families. Quite the contrary: they have large families because they are poor."[23]

The issue of space is relatively easy to deal with; the following topics are more challenging.

Food

This is the original Malthusian concern and continues to be a major worry especially in the light of recent spikes in food prices. As the population grows, so the argument goes, it will sooner or later outstrip the ability of the available land to provide the food it needs. As a result people will not have enough food to eat and will succumb to either disease or famine which would bring the population back down to a level that the land could support.

Malthus was in some senses unfortunate in his timing as precisely when he was publishing his famous essay the Agricultural Revolution was beginning to get into full swing meaning that the productivity of the land increased far faster than the increase in population and has generally continued to do so. The key difference between the Malthusians and neo-Malthusians on the one hand and those with a more optimistic view on the other is that while the former accept, although at times begrudgingly, that increases in food production have generally kept pace with, if not exceeded increases in population, they think that our good fortune is going to run out and we will not be able to continue cheating the grim reaper in this way. On the other hand the optimists see no reason why we cannot continue, with the continual application of human ingenuity, to improve food production techniques.

Paul Ehrlich also suffered from the same bad timing as Malthus. Soon after he made his statements quoted above the Green Revolution in Asia took off.

According to the United Nations Food and Agricultural Organisation, the world currently produces enough food for everybody, but many people do not have access to it.[24] Therefore problems about a lack of food are often related more to politics and local power structures than agriculture. Amartya Sen, Thomas W. Lamont University Professor and Professor of Economics and Philosophy at Harvard University and a Fellow of Trinity College Cambridge, has argued that famines very rarely if ever happen in a democracy. This is because, for example, democracies tend to be associated with a relatively free press and so if one area of a country is suffering from a famine it will be known about in the rest of the country. However, dictators can often suppress such information and may even allow, or create, famines, as a way of oppressing those parts of the population which do not support them.

Colin Clark, a professor of Agriculture in Oxford University, in the 1970s estimated that with the then known technology the world could feed over 40 billion people on a US style diet or 100 billion on a Japanese style diet.[25] Although what seems more likely is that Asians in developing economies such as China and India will start eating a more Westernised diet, particularly eating more meat, than that Western consumers will start eating a Japanese style diet although there is an increasing number of Japanese and other Asian fast food outlets in Western cities. Since Clark's time technology has developed enormously such that agricultural techniques are more efficient not just with respect to human labour but also with respect to energy and water use.

Recent concerns over insufficient food supplies have arisen partly as a result of increased demand for bio-fuels which may have contributed to a reduction in the availability of food for poor people. However, the increased demand for bio-fuels could actually help farmers in poor countries if they are able to get higher prices for their produce.

Ester Boserup, an agricultural economist, demonstrated that population pressure works, over the long run, to improve agricultural methods. She explained that initially a group would farm the easier parts of the country and only as the population increased would they start using the more difficult lands. In other words, "necessity is the mother of invention". And this is an example of an argument that also applies elsewhere: we do not really know what human beings and the Earth is capable of until the pressure is on. Ester Boserup stated that "The power of ingenuity would always outmatch that of demand". She also stated that "In fact, it is a valid generalization to say that in feudal economies the most prosperous periods are those when population is rising rapidly, and much land clearing, irrigation and terracing of hillsides is going on. In periods of rapid population increase, the desire for additional soldiers and luxuries can, more easily than in periods of stagnant population, be satisfied without depopulation of the villages and neglect of agriculture. In other words, population growth often seems to be the cause of prosperity, in sharp contrast to the causation from prosperity to population growth and poverty, which was suggested by Malthus."[26]

Using the promise of future technological advances to solve current and future food problems could be considered as dangerous wishful thinking and indeed perhaps at some point humanity could run out of new ideas. But based on past experience, and the rapid pace of technological advances in areas such as communication, which is really all we have to go on, this is unlikely to happen anytime soon. Of course new technologies are not panaceas, they need to be used responsibly. Just as nuclear power needs stringent safeguards around its use, so developments in agriculture such as Genetically Modified Crops also need to be handled with care to ensure that they really are of benefit to mankind and poor farmers in particular.

Mineral resources

One of the consequences of the ability to take photographs of the Earth from outer space is that its finiteness stands out in stark contrast to the seemingly infinitude of space. As the Earth is clearly of a fixed size then clearly there must be a finite amount of the minerals that we need in order to live, for example copper, silicon, iron. Unlike food, these minerals literally do not grow on trees. However, as pointed out above when discussing how much room we have, the Earth is actually a very large place and so the amount of certain minerals in the Earth is actually very large. In fact, for many minerals we do not know how much there is available. This is for the simple reason that we have no need to know and, as it costs money to carry out investigations mining companies only look a few years or at most decades ahead.

In addition to what is available on Earth there are also other planets and moons that could be a source of minerals – this may not be feasible for some decades or even centuries to come but who knows what human ingenuity might be able to achieve over the next 200 years?

However, when all is said and done, most people are not that interested in minerals as such. No one wants a lump of iron or copper or some 'rare earth'. They want saucepans and wires for transmitting electricity or a mobile phone. As time goes on, new materials are discovered which are better than the previous one for providing the same service. For example, optical fibres, made essentially from sand, which is abundant, can be used to replace copper wires. As well as the substitution of one mineral by another, minerals can be recycled from one use to another. This means that the available amount of a mineral is not limited to what can be dug out of the ground but also includes the supply of that mineral in items that are no longer used. The discovery and extraction of mineral deposits or mining less easily recoverable minerals depends on the cost of extraction, the price that those minerals can be sold at, technological developments and government policy, including tax rates.

A sign of whether a mineral is getting rarer or more plentiful relative to the demand for that mineral is its price. If the price increases it tends to mean that demand for that mineral is increasing compared to its supply. On the other hand if the price falls, it means that the mineral is getting less popular compared to its supply and the danger of running out of that particular mineral will have reduced. Back in 1980 Julian Simon bet Paul Ehrlich that minerals would generally fall in price. Simon allowed Ehrlich to choose whichever 5 minerals he wanted, (he chose chromium, copper, nickel, tin and tungsten), and the time period, (he chose 1980 to 1990). At the end of the 10 year period, during which the world's population increased by over 800 million, the minerals were all cheaper than at the start and Simon won the bet. This does not imply that Simon would have won the same bet with different minerals over a different time period. However, it does show that population increase is only one of the potential causes of increases in mineral prices and not necessarily a particularly strong one at that.

Some of those who express concern about population growth claim that as a result of this growth we will soon run out of certain resources. They claim that those who do not see this as a problem are naïve cornucopians, that is people who believe that continued progress and provision of material items for mankind can be met by similarly continued advances in technology. What they seem to overlook is that if resources are indeed finite, then we will run out of them sooner or later, it is just a matter of when. Therefore they too have to assume that technological developments will need to come to our rescue if disaster is to be averted.

Energy

Without a plentiful and secure source of energy, economic development will be impossible to maintain let alone achieve. The take-off of economic development in industrialised countries largely coincided with the introduction of new ways of harnessing the energy stored in coal and oil deposits.

Although coal has been used as a source of energy for heating and metal working since before the birth of Christ it was only really during the 18th century that large scale mining and usage of coal began. Up until then therefore, most energy needs were provided by renewable sources – wind, water and organic material either as food to sustain human and animal labour or wood to feed fires. As well as being more efficient than the use of wood in fires, the use of coal freed men and women from being limited in their source of energy to what they could grow. They now had access to and had the technology to make use of, the large reserves of energy contained within the coal deposits formed many centuries before. Since then the extraction and use of oil and gas deposits has provided additional energy sources. What all these sources of energy have in common is that there are, in total, large supplies. Based on recent production levels and proven reserves the world has around 120 years worth of coal available, 50 years of oil and 60 years of gas. There will though be other sources of fossil fuels that are not known about for the same reason as for sources of minerals – there is currently no need to know.

At present there is much debate about the potential effect of Carbon Dioxide (CO_2) on the environment through climate change. As the use of fossil fuels contributes to the levels of CO_2 in the atmosphere there may be environmental reasons why we ought to look at other sources of energy. I will return to environmental issues associated with population growth below.

Even if we eventually run up against declining supplies of fossil based fuels there are alternative sources, some of which are only starting to be harnessed in any significant quantities. Renewable energy sources such as solar, wind and tidal power have the potential to make a significant contribution to human energy needs. A lot of future demographic growth is expected to take place in Sub-Saharan Africa, a region with access to potentially large amounts of solar power.

There is also increasing the amount of power generated from nuclear fission and potentially from nuclear fusion processes. While there are concerns over the safety of nuclear power it is important to keep these in perspective and not use them simply as an excuse for obstructing access to these technologies.

As well as increasing the supply of energy, there is also a lot that people in richer countries can do to reduce the amount of energy they consume.

Water

Without water life would be impossible. Access to clean water is one of the key indicators of development as it makes a significant difference to the health of the population. It is natural to assume that as populations grow access to water will become harder and that sources of water will run dry. The term 'water wars' has been coined to describe what some see as the next main cause for wars, people will not fight over land or oil but over water. However, it is probably more likely that precisely because water is so important that countries will avoid going to war and will in fact negotiate settlements. An article in the 'New Statesman' on 25

March 2010 stated that "Managing increased demand [of water] in the context of increased climactic variability presents a huge challenge but if properly addressed, there is more than enough water to go round. Unlike oil, water's unique importance for human and economic development means that dependence on this shared resource generally does more to bring people together than force them apart. Historically, states sharing river courses have tended to find non-violent ways of resolving disputes and sharing the resource, and the vast majority of conflicts over water have remained confined to the local level. Over the past 50 years, more than 200 water treaties have been successfully negotiated. In a recent interview Secretary of UN-Water Nikhil Chandavarkar stated "that there are many more examples of successful transboundary cooperation than conflict over water." There are some serious and protracted conflicts, such as in Palestine or Darfur, where access to water is a major focus. However, in most cases, those conflicts are symptomatic of wider conflicts driven by deeper ethnic tensions or historic grievances."[27]

Even if there are no wars about water there is concern that there will not, for example, be enough water for irrigation. However, this is another area where one can be hopeful that future technological developments will make irrigation more efficient and also enable greater levels of recycling of water to take place. Where there is a sufficient supply of energy it is possible to desalinate sea water to provide water for agriculture and directly for human populations. One can also be hopeful that sources of water, such as the huge Nubian Sandstone Aquifer System under the Sahara desert will be made better use of.

Economic development

The relationship between population growth and economic development has been hotly disputed over the past 50 years. Similarly the question whether poor people have more children because they are poor or are they poor because they have more children has not been answered one way or the other. Up until Julian Simon wrote his book 'The Ultimate Resource', the conventional wisdom was that the faster the population growth, the slower the rate of economic development. However, Simon showed that this is not the case and that other factors such as a country's political structure can be more important. He also showed that economic development could take place over a range of different fertility levels except that below replacement fertility seemed to lead to poor long term outcomes no matter what the conditions.

Nonetheless in the short term a drop in birth rates can lead to an acceleration of economic development, the so called "demographic dividend", as it creates a window of opportunity when the proportion of the population in the working age groups is relatively large compared to the dependent population at young and older ages. However, this dividend will only be achieved in the presence of suitable political, economic and social conditions. If these are absent a country could instead end up with a 'youth bulge' of unemployed young people which could have serious adverse social and political consequences.

When someone argues that a larger population slows economic development they tend to be focusing on people purely as consumers. However, while babies arrive with a mouth they also come with a brain and two arms. What they need is the right conditions and motivations to be productive and these conditions are rarely dependent just on the demographic situation.

Economic development is usually measured in terms of national income per person. This is not a totally satisfactory measure because, as Peter Bauer pointed out, "It takes no account of the satisfaction people derive from having children or from living longer. The birth of a child immediately reduces income per head for the family and for the economy as a whole. The death of the same child has the opposite effect. Yet for most people, the first event is a blessing and the second a tragedy. Ironically, the birth of a child is registered as a reduction in national income per head while the birth of a farm animal shows up as an improvement."[28]

The environment

This final section covers the impact of population growth on the environment and includes both climate change and non-climate change related environmental issues.

When discussing environmental issues it is worth bearing in mind Pope Benedict XVI's words from his encyclical 'Caritas in Veritate': "The Church has a responsibility towards creation and she must assert this responsibility in the public sphere. In so doing, she must defend not only earth, water and air as gifts of creation that belong to everyone. She must above all protect mankind from self-destruction. There is need for what might be called a human ecology, correctly understood. The deterioration of nature is in fact closely connected to the culture that shapes human coexistence: when "human ecology" is respected within society, environmental ecology also benefits. Just as human virtues are interrelated, such that the weakening of one places others at risk, so the ecological system is based on respect for a plan that affects both the health of society and its good relationship with nature."[29]

While humans can be the cause of environmental damage they can also be the cause of environmental improvement and recovery. Much depends on the incentives and options for action. Where humans have no choice, for example, but to practice environmentally unfriendly farming methods to survive, it is not surprising that they do so. Also where ownership of environmental goods does not exist or is unclear and no one is responsible for taking care of the environment then again it would come as no surprise that the environment gets neglected – the so called 'Tragedy of the Commons'.

However, environmental concerns appear to be the latest battle ground for those who wish to see slower population growth and a smaller global population. Whereas the problems relating to the topics discussed previously, i.e. space, food, water and so on, would mainly impact the growing population, environmental issues have a potential to affect the whole population of the earth and so can be a much more affective and emotive argument for population control.

While not wishing to reduce the importance that needs to be given to environmental issues, it is important to realise that not every scare story about the reduction of rainforests, the loss of bio-diversity or the level of pollution that one might read or hear about is true. The very title of Bjorn Lomborg's book 'The Skeptical Environmentalist' indicates that one has to be careful to distinguish between fact and fiction when discussing the state, say, of the world's forests or rivers or the level of pollution. The example of species extinction is illustrative of the danger of exaggeration. In the "Global 2000 Report to the President" (in spite of its name the report was prepared at the request of US President Jimmy Carter in 1980) the authors stated that "the world faces an urgent problem of loss of plant and animal genetic resources. An estimate prepared for the Global 2000 Study suggests that between half a million and 2 million species – 15 to 20 per cent of all species on earth – could be extinguished by 2000, mainly because of loss of wild habitat but also in part because of pollution. Extinction of species on this scale is without precedent in human history." Fortunately species extinction on this scale remains unprecedented because it did not happen. Nonetheless such apocalyptic forecasts continue to be made. Species extinction is extremely hard to measure first of all because we do not actually know how many species there are and secondly the rate fluctuates widely over time. Undaunted by this difficulty, Paul Ehrlich stated "biologists don't need to know how many species there are, how they are related to one another , or how many disappear annually to recognise the Earth's biota (i.e. its flora and fauna) is entering a gigantic spasm of extinction". Not a particularly scientific approach to assessing the problem! Al Gore in his film 'An Inconvenient Truth" said that man-made global warming will cause the extinction of the polar bear in 25 years. As with other species it is difficult to count the number of polar bears in existence but the overall numbers are estimated by the International Union for Conservation of

Nature at between 20,000 and 25,000 and, while some populations of polar bear are declining, others are stable or increasing in number.

However, the biggest environmental issue relating to population is climate change. After all, if climate change is largely due to CO_2 and other emissions and if these are largely due to human activity then it would seem to make sense that an increasing population, especially if it is, at the same time, getting richer and producing more emissions, will accelerate the speed of climate change. Some authors have suggested that the cheapest way of slowing down climate change would be to increase the availability of family planning to reduce the birth rate. The authors tend to assume a simplistic relationship between the size and the wealth of a population and its level of greenhouse gas emissions ignoring the impact of technology. Under their assumptions the biggest culprits would be the USA and China. However, given the already wide availability of contraception in the USA and China's current demographic policy, increasing the availability of family planning is unlikely to make much difference to the emissions from these two countries. The same authors tend to separately argue that slower population growth is needed in order to speed up economic development. However, economic development will tend to bring with it more greenhouse gas emissions and so their plan for reducing emissions by reducing the birth rate will be self-defeating if it is offset by increased economic growth. Returning to the earlier quote from Julian Simon, the solution to climate change lies in scientific, political and cultural developments by human beings.

Some demographic terminology

Mortality rates

When we talk about mortality or death rates we usually mean what is technically called the Crude Death Rate which is simply the number of deaths in a country in a year divided by the average size of the population in that year. As mortality improves and people live longer Crude Death Rates tend to fall. However, there comes a point when, because we have to die some time, the Crude Death Rate will start increasing again as the larger number of older people start to die.

As well as the mortality rate for the total population, demographers and others are interested in mortality for specific subsets of people, particularly infant mortality rates (deaths of children below the age of 1) and maternal mortality (deaths of women during or just after pregnancy). The good news is that both infant mortality and maternal mortality are falling across the globe in richer and poorer countries. Furthermore, countries such as El Salvador, Chile, Poland, and Nicaragua, which prohibit abortion after having previously allowed it, have not seen their maternal mortality worsen. In fact, it has improved. Meanwhile, South Africa has seen mortality worsen after the legalisation of abortion. Ireland which has strict abortion laws has one of the lowest maternal mortality rates. Therefore, it is not true that where abortion is illegal there is necessarily high rates of unsafe abortion and high levels of maternal death. After all, maternal mortality fell in countries such as the UK well before abortion was made illegal. What is more important is to have trained birth attendants who can deal with any complications that might arise. However, both infant and maternal mortality in many developing countries are still relatively high compared to richer countries and this needs to be addressed.

Fertility rates

An equivalent measure to the Crude Death Rate is the Crude Birth Rate which is calculated as the number of births in a year divided by the average size of the population in that year. However, a more commonly used fertility statistic is the Total Fertility Rate (TFR) which is the average number of children a group of women born in the same year would have at the end of their reproductive period, assuming they all lived that long, if they experienced during their whole lives the fertility rates experienced in a given period (usually a year) by women of different ages. The TFR is therefore a snapshot of the current fertility experience of women. While it is widely used, it has the disadvantage that it can underestimate future fertility if women are delaying childbearing or overestimate it if women are tending to have children at earlier ages. Currently, the TFR varies from just over 7 in Niger to around 1 in Hong Kong and Macao and just over 1 in Bosnia, Slovenia and Slovakia. Countries commonly thought of as "Catholic countries", for example, Italy, Spain and Poland, also are currently experiencing low TFRs below 1.5. The UK has a TFR of around 1.9 up from a low of 1.6 in 2001, partly due to increasing fertility among over 35 year olds and partly due to recent migrants having more children on average than the indigenous population. Ireland and the USA have TFRs of just over 2.

Migration

The third demographic process that influences a country's population size and structure is migration. Migration is often a very politically sensitive issue but is something that needs to be addressed as it is one of the proposed solutions to the problems caused by ageing populations. Pope Benedict XVI in 'Caritas in Veritate' stated that "Another aspect of integral human development that is worthy of attention is the phenomenon of migration. This is a striking phenomenon because of the sheer numbers of people involved, the social, economic, political, cultural and religious problems it raises, and the dramatic challenges it poses to nations and the international community. We can say that we are facing a social

Population projections

It is worth considering population projections, such as those produced by the UN, and how reliable they are. First of all, as the UN itself points out, they are projections and not predictions. They show what would happen if a certain set of assumptions is borne out in practice. However, there is no guarantee that those assumptions will be correct, especially over the longer term. Trying to predict what the population will be in 90 years time is a risky business. At the global level, projections of future population are based on the current population and use assumptions about future mortality rates and fertility rates because at the global level migration makes no difference. Future mortality and fertility assumptions are based on current rates but allow for changes in these rates taking into account recent trends. For example, mortality rates are assumed to continue to fall in most countries even allowing for the impact of HIV/AIDS. Fertility rates are assumed to fall where they are currently considered high but there is an underlying assumption that in the long term fertility rates will tend towards the replacement level. This assumption is open to challenge as there is currently no evidence to show that fertility will return to replacement levels where it is currently below even if there has been in recent years a rise in fertility rates in some countries with the lowest levels of fertility.

The UN allows for changes in the mortality and fertility rates taking place at different speeds in different countries. The projections produced by the UN are generally relatively accurate for the decade or two after the projection was prepared but they get less accurate the further into the future they go and it is particularly the fertility assumptions that tend to differ most from actual experience. The projections may also be relatively accurate at the global level but with differences at individual country level. The accuracy of the projections also relies on the quality of the data that they are based on which, even in developed countries, is not always ideal. However, the UN projections are generally the best available and are widely used. The UN produces a number of sets of projections. In addition to the medium variant it also produces high and low variants for which it uses higher and lower fertility assumptions respectively. The most recent set of projections (the 2010 population in 2100 prospects) project a global population of 10.1 billion on the medium variant and 6.2 billion and 15.8 billion on the low and high variant projections respectively. This shows that seemingly small differences in fertility assumptions can make a big difference to projected population numbers.

A two-sided debate

In this short booklet I can do no more than scratch the surface of the debate around the various effects of population growth. My aim is not to bring to a screeching halt a debate that has been going on for over two millennia and will undoubtedly continue for quite a while yet. What I hope to have achieved is to make readers aware that there is a two-sided debate and that the population growth and higher birth rates than many countries currently have, far from being a source of problems is a solver of many problems including some of those that we face today such as ageing populations. The Catholic Church's contribution to this debate is constructive, pro-life and in tune with the aspirations of people of many cultures and deserves a fair hearing.

Endnotes

[1] Chesterton, G.K. (1904) *The Napoleon of Notting Hill Gate*.

[2] Cf. Blessed John Paul II (2001) *Novo Millenio Inuente*, 1.

[3] Cf. UN (2011) *World Population Prospects: The 2010 Revision*, http://esa.un.org/unpd/wpp/index.htm.

[4] Blessed John Paul II (1979) *Redemptor Hominis*, 14.

[5] UN Population Division (1999) *The World at Six Billion*.

[6] Cf. UN (2011) *World Population Prospects: The 2010 Revision*, http://esa.un.org/unpd/wpp/index.htm.

[7] Cf '*The Demographic Winter*' DVD www.demographicwinter.com.

[8] Cf. 7 UN (2011) *World Population Prospects: The 2010 Revision*, http://esa.un.org/unpd/wpp/index.htm.

[9] Sen A. K. (2001) *Many faces of gender inequality*. Frontline 2001; 19 November;18: 4-14.

[10] Tertullian, *De Anima*, Chapter XXX. Available at http://www.tertullian.org/fathers2/ANF-03/anf03-22.htm#P2881_991991.

[11] Machiavelli, *Discourses on the first decade of Titus Livius*, Chapter V. Available at http://www.gutenberg.org/files/10827/10827-8.txt.

[12] T. Malthus, *An Essay on the Principle of Population* (1798), Chapter VII. Available at http://www.gutenberg.org/files/4239/4239-h/4239-h.htm.

[13] Quoted in R.L. Meek, *Marx and Engels on Malthus* (Delhi: People's Publishing House, 1956).

[14] Ehrlich, Paul R. (1968). *The Population Bomb*. Ballantine Books.

[15] Simon, J. (1996). *The Ultimate Resource 2*, Princeton University Press.

[16] Pearce, F (2011), *Peoplequake*. Transworld. London p 4.

[17] Vatican Council II (1965) *Gaudium et Spes*, 50.

[18] Blessed John Paul II (1994) *Crossing the Threshold of Hope*.

[19] www.catholicnewsagency.com/archive/2004/04/07/ accessed 3 June 2011.

[20] Blessed John Paul II (1981) *Familiaris Consortio*, 30.

[21] *Catechism of the Catholic Church* No. 2372.

[22] Ehrlich, P. (1968) *The Population Bomb*.

[23] Mamdani, M. (1973) *The Myth of Population Control; Family, Caste, and Class in an Indian Village*.

[24] See FAO http://www.fao.org/hunger/faqs-on-hunger/en/#c41481 accessed 3 June 2011.

[25] Clark, C. (1967) *Population Growth and Land Use*.

[26] Boserup, E. (1965) *The Conditions of Agricultural Growth* www.biw.kuleuven.be/aee/clo/idessa_files/Boserup1965.pdf.

[27] See www.newstatesman.com/2010/03/water-access-sanitation-world accessed 3 June 2011.

[28] Bauer, P. (1998) *Population growth: disaster or blessing?* http://findarticles.com/p/articles/mi_hb3316/is_n1_v3/ai_n28707166/ accessed 3 June 2011.

[29] Benedict XVI. *Caritas in Veritate*, 51.

[30] Benedict XVI, *Caritas in Veritate*, 62.